Discovering Our Traditions

Jean Laugeay:

Fireworks and Liberty

Why We Celebrate
the Fourth of July with Fireworks

By
Denruth Lougeay, Ph.D. & Denis Lougeay

Published by
Montezuma Publishing
Aztec Shops Ltd.
San Diego State University
San Diego, California 92182-1701
619-594-7552
www.montezumapublishing.com

Denruth Lougeay, Ph.D. and Denis Lougeay
lougeay@gmail.com

ISBN: 978-1-7269-0975-4

Publishing Manager: Lia Dearborn
Production Manager: Steve Murawka
Design and Layout: Lia Dearborn

Front Cover: John Nixon giving the first public reading of the
Declaration of Independence from the steps of Independence
Hall in Philadelphia, Pennsylvania on 8 July 1776. Image ©
North Wind Pictures / Bridgeman Images.

Preface

In 2009, I was done with therapy clients for the day when my youngest son, Gregg, sent an email containing several old newspaper clippings. Accompanying the clippings was a note that referenced my life-long passion for family genealogy. The advertisements within his note featured a name so similar to our earliest-known ancestor (who was also from Philadelphia) that Gregg thought I just might be interested. Gregg wrote that the ads seemed to be about "a fireworks guy during the early revolutionary period." Hmmm... the search had begun!

Here we are, fifteen years later, having conducted original research and taken extensive trips both within the United States and abroad, leaving no stone unturned. We wish to share the remarkable story of Jean Laugeay and his patriotism with our sons, Stace and Gregg, and the generations that follow. We also wish to reveal this historical perspective of pyrotechnic history with all Americans and anyone who has experienced the thrill of fireworks.

Since I was a little girl, I have vivid memories of brilliant and magical fireworks...never knowing that I would marry into the family that began this wonderful American tradition. I never imagined that I would be the family genealogist who would reveal the history and legacy of this man, Jean Laugeay. It seems strange to me that his name and legacy at a key point in US history has been unknown for almost 250 years. Thanks to this discovery, we now know Jean's pivotal role in celebrating the first anniversary of the signing of the Declaration of Independence on the Fourth of July in 1777. And what follows is his story.

—Denruth Lougeay
Author and Family Genealogist

John Adams inspired it...
Jean Laugeay made it happen...

Contents

The Declaration of Independence is Signed

It is July 8, 1776. Jean is gently leaning against the Franklin lamppost with his arms encircling the lamppost itself. He is feeling excited, though lightheaded and almost breathless. While Philadelphia can be hot and humid midsummer, this particular year is unseasonably mild. Jean is intent on every word being read that morning at the State House (which later becomes Independence Hall). John Nixon, a leader in the patriot cause, is officially reading each word of the newly created Declaration of Independence and proclaiming freedom from the rapacious King George III of the British homeland (*Front Cover Image*).

What Jean hears is almost too good to be true. The words are magic to his ears. The concept of liberty and self-rule is frequently sought by mankind, but rarely achieved for any substantial duration. Could it be true that all men would be equal, instead of their lot in life being predetermined and subject to the rules of royalty? Could the citizens actually self-govern? These ideals are unprecedented, yet they are being proposed by many of the most successful and respected leaders of the Thirteen Colonies. Furthermore, although they have the most to lose, these 56 architects of a new world are preparing to sign this document, and they are pledging their lives, their fortunes, and their sacred honor.

Born in France

Jean Baptiste Laugeay (jhon law-jháy) is born on September 28, 1736, in Orignolles, Charente-Maritime, Poitou-Charentes, France, which is in the Bordeaux region. He is baptized at the Saint Martin d Ary Church (*Figure 1, inside front cover*), north of St. Emillion in the Cognac area (*Figure 2*).

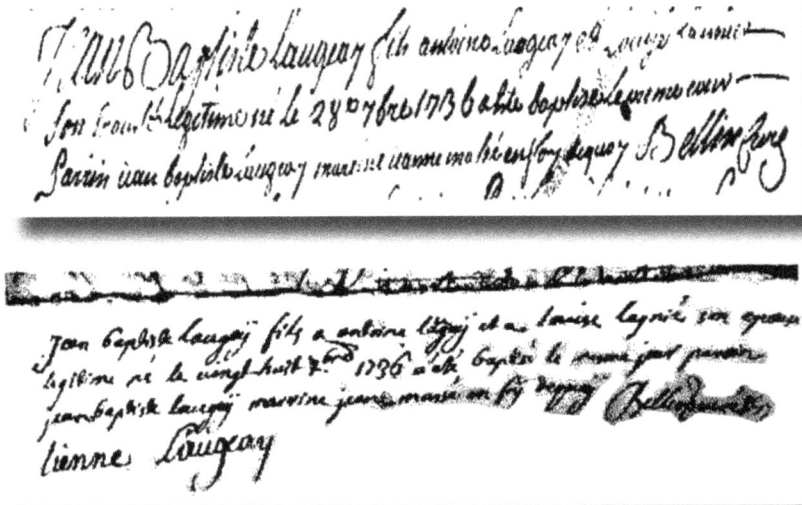

Figure 2. Baptismal certificates, Church of Saint Martin d Ary, Orignolles, Charente-Maritime, Poitou-Charentes, France: Jean Baptiste Laugeay, son of Antoine Laugeay and Louise Launier, is born on 28th of September in 1736 and baptized the same day. Godfather Jean Baptiste Laugeay and Godmother Jeanne Masse. (From two different church books).

In 1723, his parents, Antoine Laugeay and Louise Lanier, had married a few miles away, at the church of Saint Gilles in Chalaux (*Figure 3*). Jean's surviving siblings are Etienne (b. 1725) and Marguerite (b. 1731). Etienne serves as a notary for the townspeople of Orignolles on many documents that exist today.

Figure 3. Marriage certification of Antoine Laugeay and Louise Lanier at the Church of Saint Gilles of Chalaux in February 1723.

There is scant record of Jean's youth in southwest France. Jean is a winemaker in his early days. As a young man, he serves in the French Army where he learns the "Art of Artificial Fire Works" (*Figure 4*). Although he is baptized in the Catholic Church, it is very likely that Jean becomes a Huguenot. An estimated ten percent of the French population is Huguenot. They are Protestants who were often persecuted during the sixteenth through eighteenth centuries and, as a result, emigrated to seek liberty in other countries. Jean is most likely one of them, as indicated by where his presence is next discovered.

JEAN LAUGEAY, MAKER OF ARTIFICIAL FIRE WORKS, OFFERS HIS SERVICES TO CONGRESS IN 1776.

The Journal of Congress for August 28th, 1776, records a petition from Jean Laugeay presented to Congress and read. The Petition stated:

To the Honorable The Continental Congress,

Honorable Sirs: Your Petitioner Jean Laugeay, French Man, has been brought up to the Art of Artificial Fire Works in France; an Art so necessary to make Signals and render lights, both to the Navies, and Armies in Camp, at the time of Night, as to be looked upon by most Nations in Europe as a considerable Branch of the Art of War; the Importunes [Importance] whereof being so little known in this part of the World, has induced the Petitioner to offer his Service to the Honorable the Continental Congress of America; to be employed by them in the Art of Fire Works, and in such a Station as they may on enquiring into his Character and abilities judge him most capable of.

Should This Honourable House think proper to employ the Petitioner in Their service, he shall by every Means in his Power endeavor to discharge the Duty entrusted to him with every mark of Honesty and Fidelity. I am. Honorable Sirs, With the Utmost Duty & Respect,

Your most obedient and Most Humble Servant,

[Signed] JEAN LEAUGEAY.

From the Papers of the Continental Congress, No. 42, IV folio 96

Figure 4. Jean Laugeay wrote to the Continental Congress on August 28, 1776, the month following the first reading of the Declaration of Independence in Philadelphia. He offers his services "in the Art of Fire Works."

Immigration to Ireland

By 1760, at the age of 24, Jean has left France and is living in Ireland. When Jean arrives in Dublin, nonconformist Huguenots have been granted freedom of worship, and there are four Huguenot churches in Dublin. Dublin has grown to over 60,000 and has become, both socially and economically, the second most important city in Great Britain after London.

Jean joins St. Mary's Chapel for Huguenots, which is within the St. Patrick's Catholic Cathedral of Dublin. He meets his wife, Ann Boutin, a widow whose husband, Jean Boutin, died in 1757. Jean marries Ann in January 1761. Ann is usually known as Jeanne but eventually is buried as Jane.

Six children are born to the couple (Antoine, b. 1761; twins Anne and Martha, b. 1763; Jeanne, b. 1764; Jean II, b. 1766; and Anne, b. 1769). All four daughters die at a young age. At this time, George III has become King of Great Britian, and there is unrest between the Protestant and Catholic populations. Some combination of these factors likely spurs Jean, Jeanne, and their son(s) to migrate to the New World to seek opportunity.

Enterprise in the New World

Around 1771, at age 35, Jean and his family are living in Philadelphia when his daughter Jane is born. Philadelphia is the largest city in all of the colonies with a population of 40,000 and contains the State House of Pennsylvania. It is also home to a large number of influential and enterprising people whose ideas of liberty and freedom are in their infancy and growing.

In January 1772, Jean places an advertisement (one of many) in Ben Franklin's *Pennsylvania Gazette*. He promotes his desire to grow vines for gentlemen (for winemaking), announcing that his expertise was learned in the wine regions of France (*Figure 5*).

This is a substantial advertisement, detailing Jean's knowledge of assessing soil suitable for growing grapes, planting, cultivating, pruning the vines, and projecting the yield from 10 acres of land in five years. At this time, he begins to use both "Jean" and "John" as his first name but always retains the name Laugeay.

In 1773, Jean is featured as the firework inventor in a notice touting a "grand and magnificent firework superior to anything of the kind ever shown here" (*Figure 6*). About a dozen different types of displays are mentioned, totaling well over 100 individual devices. The event will be held at a private home on the Commons and will culminate with a display depicting two opposing forts, one English and one French, firing 12 cannons at each other until the English are victorious. This is the first of numerous events that will take place over the next 21 years.

JOHN LAUGEAY, late from Bourdeaux, Having had upwards of 20 years experience in planting and cultivating all the various species of VINES, at Bourdeaux, Orleans, Champagne, &c. in France, takes this method to acquaint the public, that he would be glad to engage with any Gentlemen in that capacity; and from his favourable opinion of the soil of this province, will give assurance (under Providence) to clear in five years time, from 10 acres of suitable ground, Four Hundred Pounds sterling, and upwards.

Any person desirous of conferring with the said Laugeay on this head, are requested not to delay, as the season is near at hand, when some preparations should be made. And in the interim would be glad to be employed in pruning gentlemens Vines and Fruit-trees, being a proficient therein. He will engage on very moderate terms; and for suitable satisfaction for his time and trouble, will attend any gentleman to view and give his judgement on any parcel of land, by applying to him, at his house in Seventh-street, next door to the Silk Manufactory.

Figure 5. Pennsylvania Gazette, January 23, 1772. Jean reaches out to work with gentlemen to grow their vines for wine given his twenty years' experience in France.

Historical documents from the colonial period are incomplete, and early American newspapers are sporadic at best. Yet Jean is mentioned over a dozen known times during his life in Philadelphia newspapers as well as various colonial records during the 1770s and 1780s.

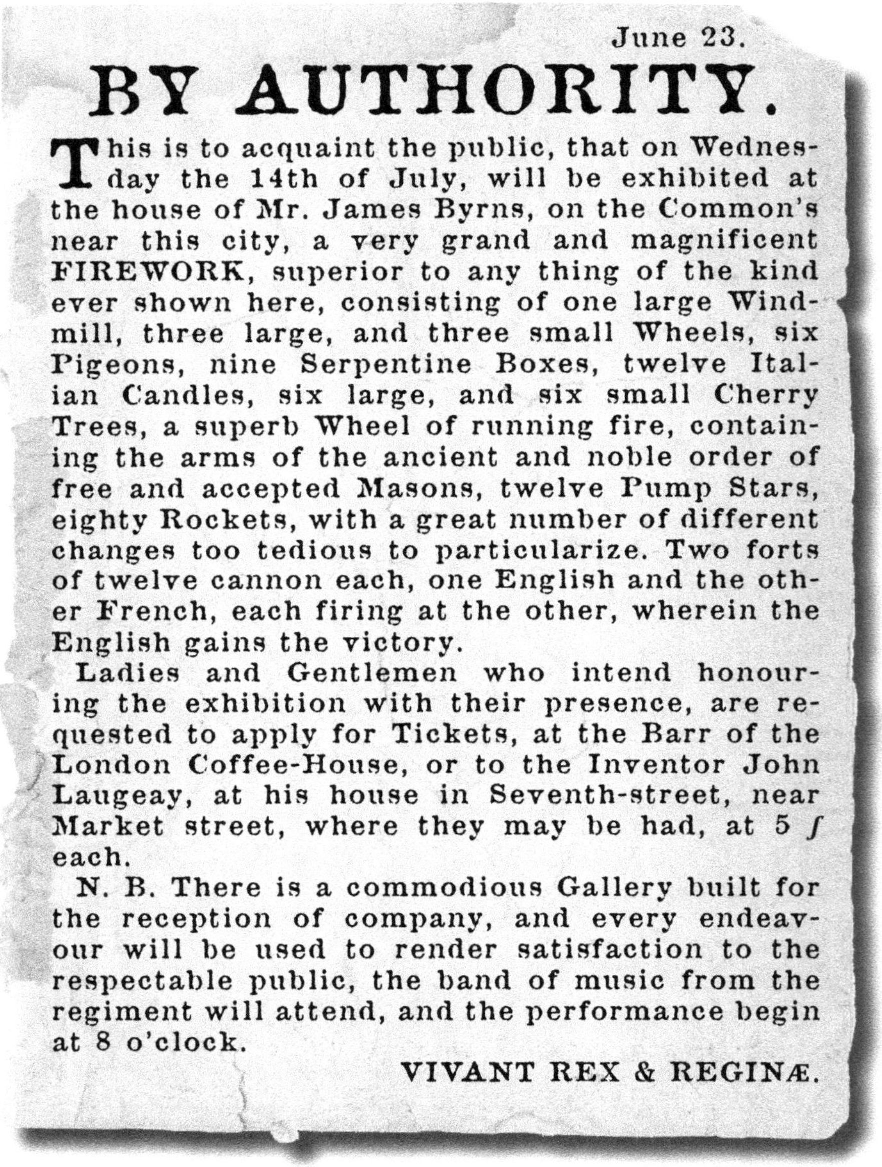

June 23.

BY AUTHORITY.

This is to acquaint the public, that on Wednesday the 14th of July, will be exhibited at the house of Mr. James Byrns, on the Common's near this city, a very grand and magnificent FIREWORK, superior to any thing of the kind ever shown here, consisting of one large Windmill, three large, and three small Wheels, six Pigeons, nine Serpentine Boxes, twelve Italian Candles, six large, and six small Cherry Trees, a superb Wheel of running fire, containing the arms of the ancient and noble order of free and accepted Masons, twelve Pump Stars, eighty Rockets, with a great number of different changes too tedious to particularize. Two forts of twelve cannon each, one English and the other French, each firing at the other, wherein the English gains the victory.

Ladies and Gentlemen who intend honouring the exhibition with their presence, are requested to apply for Tickets, at the Barr of the London Coffee-House, or to the Inventor John Laugeay, at his house in Seventh-street, near Market street, where they may be had, at 5 ʃ each.

N. B. There is a commodious Gallery built for the reception of company, and every endeavour will be used to render satisfaction to the respectable public, the band of music from the regiment will attend, and the performance begin at 8 o'clock.

VIVANT REX & REGINÆ.

Figure 6. Pennsylvania Journal, June 23, 1773. Jean mentions eleven-plus types of fireworks in his current display. Note that in 1773 he states "long live the king and queen" of Britian three years prior to the drafting of the Declaration of Independence.

Jean Langeay and the Continental Congress

The Continental Congress votes for independence from Great Britain on the second of July in 1776. The next day, delegate John Adams writes a letter to his wife, Abigail, saying the day "ought to be solemnized with Pomp and Parade, with Shews [sic], Games, Sports, Guns, Bells, Bonfires and Illuminations from one End of this Continent to the other from this Time forward forever more."

The Declaration of Independence is formally approved by Congress on July 4th, and broadsheets are ordered to be sent out to the new states. The newspaper *Pennsylvania Evening Post* is the first to publish the Declaration, on July 6th, with the final signatures of most delegates gathered on August 2nd. The first official reading to the citizenry occurs that fine eighth day in July of 1776. As a resident of downtown Philadelphia, Jean likely welcomes the news with his whole heart and being...and probably immense trepidation. Jean lives and works and prays within blocks of the State House. Jean, living and working in a small community, has likely come to know many of the delegates to the Continental Congress.

Shortly before his 40th birthday, in the month following the drafting of the Declaration of Independence, Jean offers his knowledge of fireworks and his services to the Continental Congress (*Figure 4*). He states that he is a maker of artificial fireworks and that fireworks are used by navies and armies in Europe as a "considerable Branch of the Art of War." He proposes the use of fireworks to illuminate battlefields at night and to send signals for battle communication.

The petition is read to the Continental Congress on August 28th, 1776. The extent to which Jean's fireworks are actually utilized in battle during the subsequent seven years of the Revolutionary War is not known. The military would have had a strong desire to keep specific activities and signals from the British, so it is not surprising that records do not exist.

On the Fourth of July in 1777, Philadelphia commemorates the first anniversary of the Declaration of Independence. According to the *Philadelphia Evening Post*, it is celebrated "with demonstrations of joy and festivity" (*Figure 7*). It includes ships lining the Delaware River firing 13 cannon shots honoring the 13 states that have declared their independence. It features an elegant dinner with entertainment and many toasts to independence and freedom.

Each toast is followed by music and the discharge of artillery and small arms fire. The celebrations end with the ringing of bells and "a grand exhibition of fireworks (which began and concluded with thirteen rockets) on the Commons, and the city was beautifully illuminated." "Thus may the fourth of July, that glorious and memorable day, be celebrated through America, by the sons of freedom, from age to age till time shall be no more. Amen and amen."

During the winter of 1777, the British occupied Philadelphia in relative comfort. Just twenty miles away the Continental troops were camped in hastily built huts and cabins without heat during the frigid weather at Valley Forge. Tories welcomed the British to Philadelphia with open arms. Patriots fled the city. Quakers and

PHILADELPHIA.

Yesterday the 4th of July, being the Anniversary of the Independance of the United States of America, was celebrated in this
city with demonstrations of joy and festivity. About noon all the
armed ships and gallies in the river were drawn up before the
city, dressed in the gayest manner, with the colours of the United
States and streamers displayed. At one o'clock, the yards being
properly manned, they began the celebration of the day by a
discharge of thirteen cannon from each of the ships, and one
from each of the thirteen gallies, in honor of the Thirteen United
States.

In the afternoon an elegant dinner was prepared for Congress,
to which were invited the President and Supreme Executive
Council, and Speaker of the Assembly of this state, the General
Officers and Colonels of the army, and strangers of eminence,
and the Members of the several Continental Boards in town. The
Hessian band of music, taken in Trenton the 26th of December
last, attended and heightened the festivity with some fine per-
formances suited to the joyous occasion, while a corps of British
deserters, taken into the service of the continent by the state of
Georgia, being drawn up before the door, filled up the intervals
with feux de joie. After dinner a number of toasts were drank,
all breathing independance, and a generous love of liberty, and
commemorating the memories of those brave and worthy patriots who gallantly exposed their lives, and fell gloriously in
defence of freedom and the righteous cause of their country.

Each toast was followed by a discharge of artillery and small
arms, and a suitable piece of music by the Hessian band.

The glorious fourth of July was reiterated three times, accom-
panied with triple discharges of cannon and small arms, and loud
huzzas that resounded from street to street through the city. To-
wards evening several troops of horse, a corps of artillery, and
a brigade of North-Carolina forces, which was in town on its
way to join the grand army, were drawn up in Second-street,
and reviewed by Congress and the General Officers. The evening
was closed with the ringing of bells, and at night there was a
grand exhibition of fireworks (which began and concluded with
thirteen rockets) on the Commons, and the city was beautifully
illuminated. Everything was conducted with the greatest order
and decorum, and the face of joy and gladness was universal.

Thus may the fourth of July, that glorious and ever memorable day, be celebrated through America, by the sons of freedom,
from age to age till time shall be no more. Amen, and amen.

*Figure 7. The Pennsylvania Evening Post, Saturday, July 5,
1777. The celebration in Philadelphia of the first anniversary of
American independence.*

others preferred to remain neutral. A common practice at that time was that the capture of a government headquarters would end the war. That did not occur.

Approximately fifteen thousand British replaced the patriots who had fled. The occupation was difficult for those residents who remained. There were apparently no atrocities, such as mass executions and torture of common citizens. A common language and customs reduced the animosity. A desire to recruit reinforcements, plus the hope to reunite the Colonies under the British Crown, likely led to better treatment.

But prisoners of the British were beaten, starved, and provided no heat or blankets during the winter. Many prisoners and people in poverty died from starvation and sickness due to unsanitary conditions. Independence Hall was turned into a barracks and hospital. Looting and crimes by British soldiers were rampant, although not officially sanctioned. The British required letters to be sent unsealed.

How Jean experienced the British occupation is unknown, but it is likely that the British confiscated or destroyed his fireworks and supplies. It is also probable that the British negatively impacted the living conditions of Jean and his family during their occupation. The French alliance with the Colonies in February of 1778 gave Jean another motivation to fight the British. He made a decision of defiance to the Crown.

In Valley Forge from April through June 1778, Jean serves under Captain Benjamin Bartholomew's Pennsylvania 5th Regiment of the Continental Army (*Figure 8*). He is on the revolutionary muster rolls as late as September 1780 (*Figure 9*). During Jean's service, the Pennsylvania 5th participates in the Battle of Monmouth

VALLEY FORGE
Muster Roll

Last Name: **Laughny**   First Name: **John**

ID: **PA23913**

Rank: **Private**   Rank Type: **Rank and File**

State: **Pennsylvania**

Regiment: **5th Pennsylvania**

Regiment Commander: **Col Francis Johnson**

Brigade: **2nd Pennsylvania**   Division: **2nd**

Division Commander: **MG Thomas Mifflin**

Company Commander: **Capt. Benjamin Bartholomew**

Comments for DEC 1777:

Comments for JAN, FEB, MAR 1778:

Comments for APR 1778: **On Guard**

Comments for MAY 1778: **Name On Roll Without Comment**

Comments for JUN 1778: **Name On Roll Without Comment**

Figure 8. Information from the Valley Forge Muster Roll for Jean Laugeay.

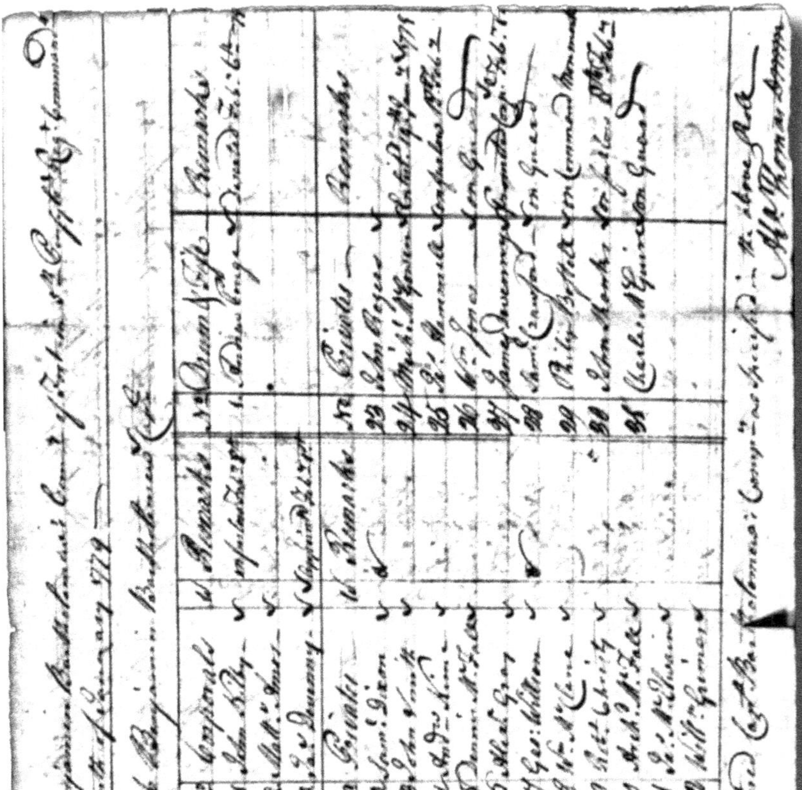

Figure 9. John Lougeay (#2 above) is a soldier in
Pennsylvania's Fifth Regiment. This is one of many muster
rolls documenting his service.

as the Colonists inflict heavy casualties on British forces withdrawing from Philadelphia via New Jersey. This battle enhances the morale of the Colonists through the belief that they could prevail. It also increases foreign support for the American effort.

On July I, 1779, Jean sends a second letter to the Continental Congress (*Figure 10*). Jean addresses the "Honorable Congress before whom I have had the Honor of exhibiting Fire Works on the like Occasion." Jean tells the Continental Congress that he would like to display fireworks to celebrate the "glorious Emancipation of this happy Land," and he indicates that he has "ready a large collection of various sorts." The fireworks display takes place after dinner at the City Tavern on July 4, 1779. It is significant that Jean is concurrently serving in the Pennsylvania 5th Regiment.

This letter continues to reveal Jean's proud patriotism and excitement, specifically through the choice of words. With reference to the Declaration of Independence, he states that "Commemorating great and important events has been an established Custom in all Nations, in all Ages." Jean writes that "the Auspicious Harbinger of America, first usher'd [sic] in the pleasing prospect of securing Happiness," and it "ought ever to be acknowledged with Gratitude as a celestial Blessing and annually celebrated with effusive Joy by the inhabitants of the United States to the End of time."

Although John Adams made similar statements to his wife upon approval of the Declaration of Independence, expressing that he desires illumination to celebrate, Jean Laugeay not only executes the concept,

That Jean Laugeay was engaged by Congress to display Fire Works at a July Fourth celebration is shown by his petition of 1779-

To His Excellency the President and the Hon'ble Representatives of the United States in Congress assembled:

*M*ay it please the Honorable Congress, Commemorating great and important Events has been an established Custom in all Nations, in all Ages.

The noble emulous Spirit it infuses and the happy Influence it generates in the minds of succeeding Generations often produce Actions that prove very beneficial to the People who practice it. Heaven certainly approves; for none but Tyrants wish to suppress it.

The glorious Emancipation of this happy Land, on the ever memorable fourth day of July, 1776, stands foremost in Magnitude and Admiration, in the Annals of the World.

That great and remarkable Era, the auspicious Harbinger of America, first usher'd in the pleasing prospect of securing Happiness to our latest posterity; and ought ever to be acknowledged with Gratitude as a celestial Blessing, and annually celebrated with effusive Joy by the inhabitants of the United States to the End of time.

Presuming with some degree of Confidence that it would be agreeable to the Honorable Congress, before whom I have had the Honor of exhibiting Fire Works on the like Occasion, I have got ready a large Collection of various sorts significantly designed, for part of the Celebration of the approaching Anniversary of our freedom and Independence. I therefore humbly pray that the Honorable Congress would be graciously pleased to signify their Approbation of my Design, by ordering me to exhibit the same on Monday Evening next, at such place as you may be pleased to appoint. Any directions the Honorable Congress shall give relative to the Exhibition I will faithfully observe and execute.

I have the honor to be with the most profound Respect and Deference. Your Excellency's & your Honours much obliged and devoted Humble Servant

[Signed] JEAN LAUGEAY.
Fire Worker.
Philadelphia, July 1st, 1779.

Figure 10. Jean Laugeay sends a second letter to the Continental Congress on July 1, 1779. It is a communication with flourish and high praise for liberty and freedom of this new country.

but also makes it a tradition that Americans celebrate to this day.

After Jean's 1779 Independence Day fireworks display, a third letter seeks reimbursement for costs of the "Anniversary of the Freedom and Independence of the United States" celebration (*Figure 11*). This letter to the Congress by Jean states "being a poor man and having a family depending for support on what I can earn by my knowledge and ingenuity in this art."

History documents the Continental Congress' struggle to pay the troops and the inability to properly supply soldiers camped at Valley Forge. Jean experiences this while trying to collect for his expenses. Documents show that his request is hotly debated by two Continental Congress delegates from South Carolina, Mr. William Henry Drayton and Mr. Henry Laurens.

Mr. Drayton supports the payment to Jean, noting that it is common "practice of all nations ancient and modern to celebrate particular days by festivity." Mr. Laurens counters and expresses "astonishment at the conduct of his honorable colleague." He references a letter stating, "all the Rich Planters in the south were ruined." He cites a "very alarming letter from the capital quarter Master General" and references currency concerns. Insults continue, indicating a major disagreement about an "anniversary" expense that would increase "the already intolerable burthen of Taxes."

Jean's third letter is also replicated, to show the handwriting at that time and Jean's original signature (*Figure 12*). All of Jean's letters are filled with emotion. He is a new immigrant to the colonies with a grand

To his Excellency the President & the Honourable Members of Congress:

The Petition of Jean Laugeay, Fire Worker, Most respectfully & humbly sheweth, That on the evening of the Day appointed for celebrating the late Anniversary of the Freedom and Independence of the United States, your Petitioner had the honour to exhibit a large Collection of fireworks, which he had prepared for that Occasion.

That the Materials, Composition, & Exhibition were attended with considerable Expence and trouble.

That your Petitioner being a poor Man and having a family solely depending for support on what he can earn by his knowledge and Ingenuity in this Art, he takes Liberty of applying to the Honorable Congress humbly begging that they would be pleased to give Orders for payment to your Petitioner of the Amount of the Expence he has been at on this occasion, or of such Sum as to the Honorable Congress may seem proper, And your Petitioner as in Gratitude bound, will ever pray for the prosperity and Happiness of the United States, &c.

[Signed] JEAN LAUGEAY.

Philadelphia, July 23d, 1779.

From the Papers of the Continental Congress, No. 42, IV. folio 204.

Figure 11. Jean Laugeay requests payments from the Continental Congress for exhibiting fireworks on the Fourth of July, 1779.

display of hope and dreams, like most who have come to America...both then and now. French Huguenots were often from an educated class. Jean's letters to Congress reveal a man of intelligence who is articulate and possesses a masterful vocabulary. Jean's expressive signatures appear to be consistent on the three letters to the Continental Congress.

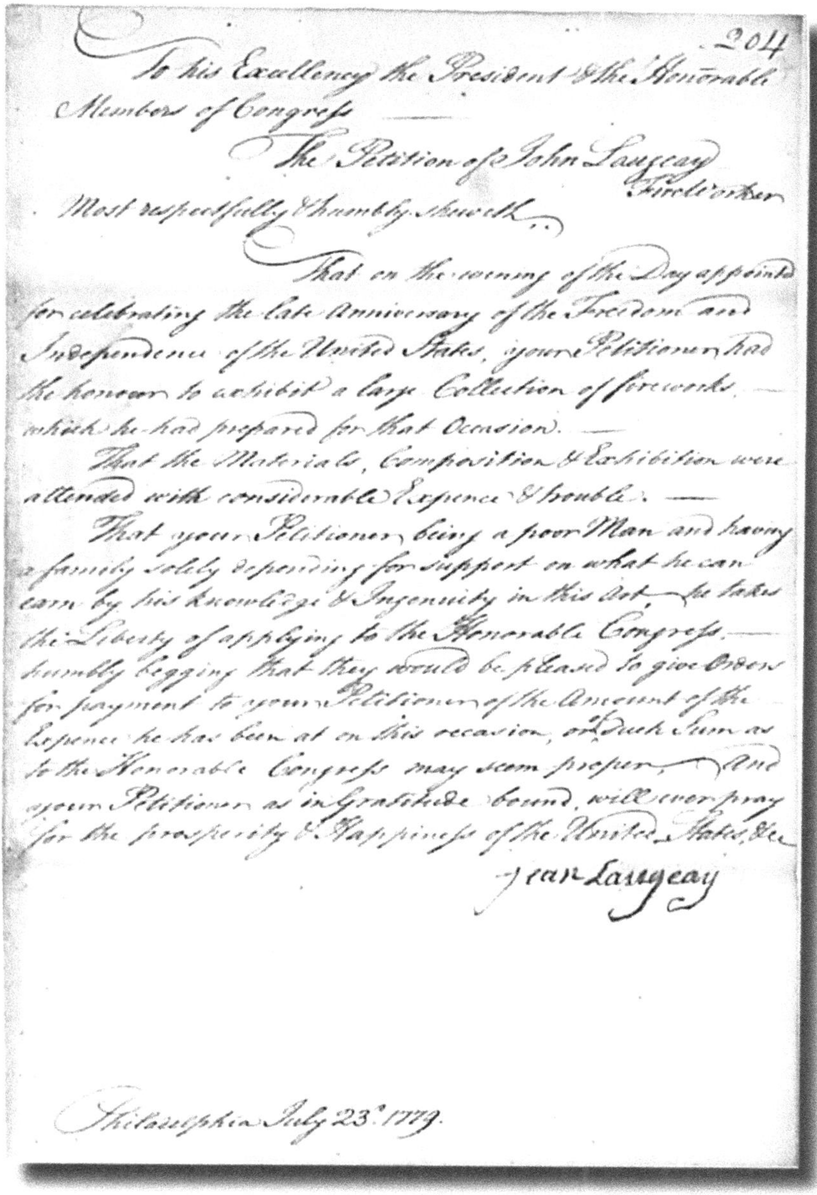

Figure 12. Jean Laugeay writes elegant letters to the Continental Congress. He requests money for his family in the summer of 1779. The original letter is included to display the elaborate handwriting of the time.

Philadelphia and the Revolutionary War

The places Jean mentioned in newspapers for fireworks displays or to purchase fireworks can be seen on a map of downtown Philadelphia (*Figure 13*). Included are also Jean Laugeay's residences on Seventh Street, Elmsley's Alley, and South Alley, as well as the locations where he held displays including at the City Tavern. All are within close proximity of the State House and St Paul's Church.

St. Paul's Episcopal Church (the primary church that Jean's family attended), was built in 1761 and still stands three blocks away from Independence Hall. The Church is located at 225 S. 3rd Street, in the Society Hill neighborhood. Jean's son, Antoine Laugeay, is buried in the Church courtyard (as Anthony Lougeay) with his wives Laomi and Phebe. Jean's residence on Elmsley Alley is in the same block as the church and is frequently mentioned in newspaper advertisements.

Thomas Paine wrote the famous tract *Common Sense* in October 1776 just next door to St. Paul's Church, to the north. Jean's wife is buried a few blocks away at St. Peter's Church. Only Dock Street lies between St. Paul's Church and the City Tavern (138 South Second Street at Walnut). Jean often refers to the tavern in his newspaper ads.

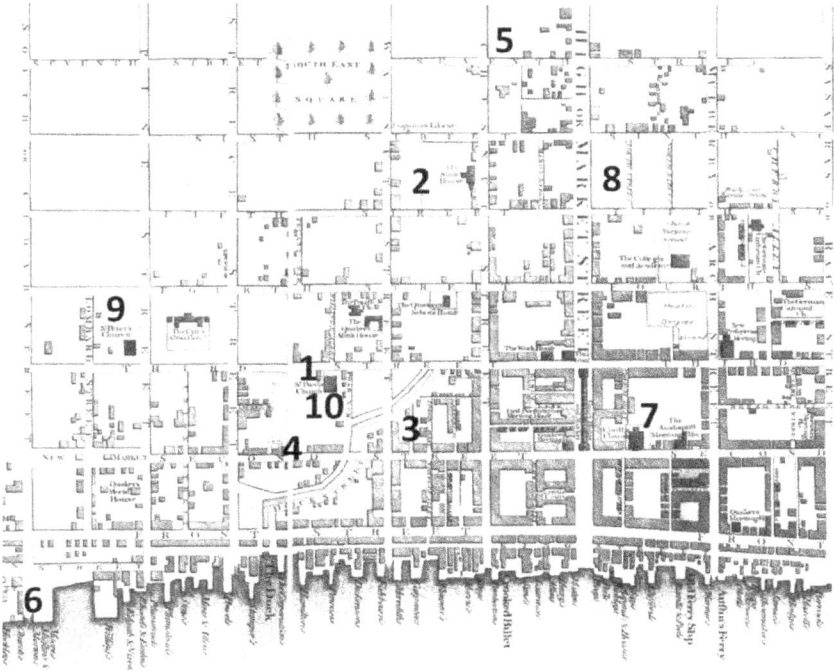

Figure 13. City of Philadelphia, 1776, The Capital of Pennsylvania Survey, by Benjamin Easbury. Amazon: Historic Map, LLC.

Map Legend

1. St Paul's Church
2. The State House/Independence Hall
3. City Tavern
4. Jean Laugeay-Elmsley Alley Residence
5. Jean Laugeay-Seventh Street House
6. Jean Laugeay Warehouse
7. Christ's Church
8. Anthony Lougeay Residence
9. Burial Site of Jean Laugeay's Wife Jane at St. Peter's Episcopal Church
10. Burial Site of Anthony Lougeay/Wives at St. Paul's Episcopal Church

The City Tavern

Just as Philadelphia was the nucleus of the Continental Congress, the City Tavern was the nucleus of Philadelphia. The City Tavern provided food, drink, and lodging for the political, social, and commercial activities of the new United States. Through its doorway entered the great men of Colonial America. General George Washington, John Adams, Benjamin Franklin, Thomas Jefferson, and Paul Revere all ate, drank, and conversed there. The Continental Congress delegates are known to have frequented the beloved City Tavern.

Jean most likely takes meals at the historic City Tavern. One can imagine that Franklin and Jean might be discussing topics of common interest there. Jean frequently advertises in Franklin's *Pennsylvania Gazette*. They share a small area of city blocks in downtown Philadelphia as their living environment, and Franklin, too, has a strong interest in science. Discussions may center on pyrotechnics, electricity, and how things work. With Franklin becoming a diplomat to France in 1776, one can presume conversations about French customs and wine since Jean is a viticulturist.

Why Are Fireworks So Fascinating?

Fireworks were developed in the second century BC in Liuyang, China. The first natural "firecrackers" were bamboo stalks that, when thrown in a fire, would explode with a bang because of the overheating of the hollow air pockets in the bamboo. The Chinese believed these natural firecrackers would ward off evil spirits. It is thought that about a 1,000 years later, a Chinese alchemist mixed potassium nitrate, sulfur, and charcoal to produce a black, flakey powder—the first "gunpowder." This powder was poured into hollowed out bamboo sticks (and later stiff paper tubes), forming the first manmade fireworks.

While firework displays were conducted in many European countries, the Italians developed them into an elaborate art form in the period 1400–1500. Then France made great advances in pyrotechnics during the reign of Louis XIV and Louis XV (1710–1774) as they encouraged grand fireworks exhibitions and expended large sums of money on them. The Ruggieri brothers (Italians who became naturalized Frenchmen) conducted many of these French displays to celebrate various events, such as royal births, marriages, and military victories. This is the environment in which Jean served in the French military and honed his pyrotechnic knowledge and abilities (*Figure 4*).

If you were there for America's first anniversary, you would not have seen multicolored fireworks. Although this was a limitation, the fireworks were a creative and inventive way to delight the crowd. Included in Jean's firework displays (*Figure 6*) were pigeons, wheels, windmills, serpentine boxes, Italian candles, cherry trees, pump stars, and rockets. Even a wheel of running fire with arms of Free Masons was offered.

Such displays must have thrilled those who had never previously witnessed any such spectacle. Jean's fireworks would have been a brilliant orange but still amazing for all who viewed them! Fireworks of other colors would not be created for another sixty years, when Italian inventors added metals such as strontium and barium in the 1830s.

The Legacy of Jean Laugeay

At the end of the Revolutionary War, Jean produces a large quantity of superior fireworks to celebrate the victory (*Figure 14*). He states that he "has exhibited (fireworks) those 13 years past in most parts of the continent". It appears that Jean is known far beyond Philadelphia for his expertise.

FIREWORKS.

Ladies and Gentlemen,

JOHN LAUGEAY, in Emley's-alley, back of St. Paul's church, Philadelphia) Artificer, who has exhibited these 13 years past in most parts of the continent, begs leave to inform the Ladies and Gentlemen, that he has now prepared, a large Quantity of Fire Works, superior to any yet made here, and is ready to exhibit the same upon the shortest notice, to any number of Ladies and Gentlemen who please to employ him on the glorious Commemeration of Peace. Those who it does not suit to send for him, may be supplied with all the various Kinds of Fire Works, properly packed up. Enquire as above.
Philadelphia, Jan. 12.

Figure 14. Pennsylvania Packet, January 12, 1784. Jean Laugeay's services reach out to "most parts of the continent."

Jean continues to display fireworks in Philadelphia for a wide variety of celebrations, including observing the nation's 11th anniversary on the Fourth of July in 1787 (*Figure 15*). At that time in history, Jean's

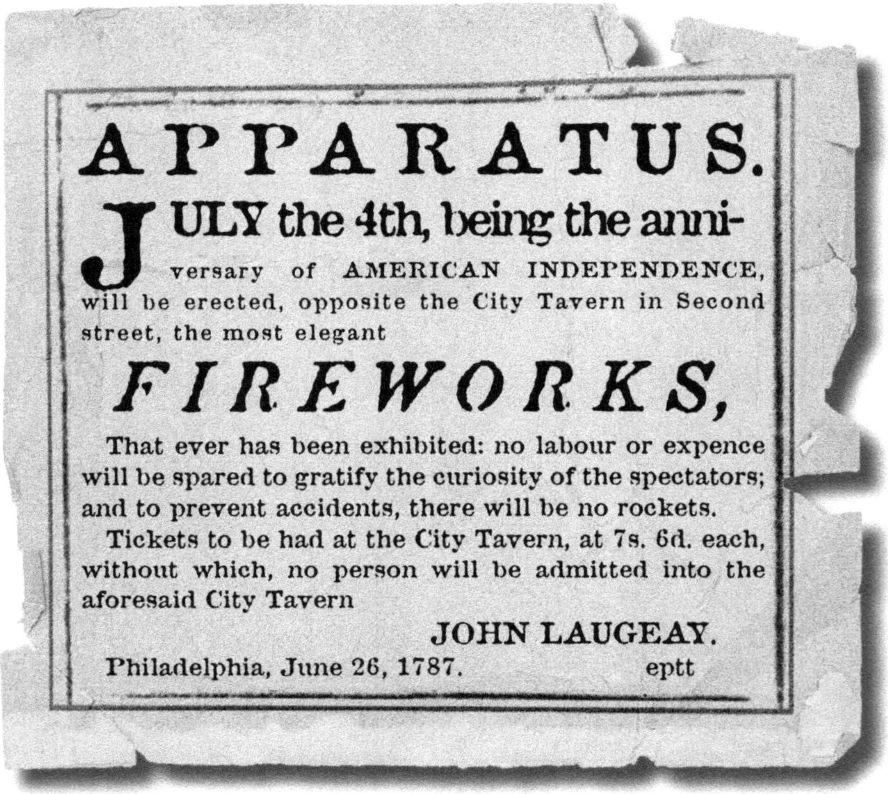

APPARATUS.

JULY the 4th, being the anniversary of AMERICAN INDEPENDENCE, will be erected, opposite the City Tavern in Second street, the most elegant

FIREWORKS,

That ever has been exhibited: no labour or expence will be spared to gratify the curiosity of the spectators; and to prevent accidents, there will be no rockets.

Tickets to be had at the City Tavern, at 7s. 6d. each, without which, no person will be admitted into the aforesaid City Tavern

JOHN LAUGEAY.

Philadelphia, June 26, 1787. eptt

Figure 15. Pennsylvania Packet, June 26, 1787. Jean Laugeay advertises Independence Day fireworks to be displayed at the famous City Tavern.

knowledge of the pyrotechnics industry was preeminent. He used at least four newspapers to advertise his fireworks events from 1773 until his death in 1794. During that period, no evidence of another fireworks person is found in the Philadelphia area.

In February of 1792, Jeanne, Jean's wife of 31 years, dies and is buried in St. Peter's Episcopal Church in Philadelphia as Jane Laugeay. Later, in October of 1792, a notice in the *Philadelphia Gazette* indicates that mail is left at the post office for Jean Laugeay.

During 1793, the deadly yellow fever was rampant in Philadelphia, killing one in fifty Philadelphia residents. Jean's home and business of many years were located on Elmsley Alley, near the docks where mosquitos thrived. At that time, it was not known that mosquitos were spreading the disease.

Then, on the 5th of August in 1794, the *Philadelphia Gazette* notes, "Departed this life on the 14th July last, in Baltimore, after a few days illness, Mr. John Laugeay, late of Philadelphia." (*Figure 16*).

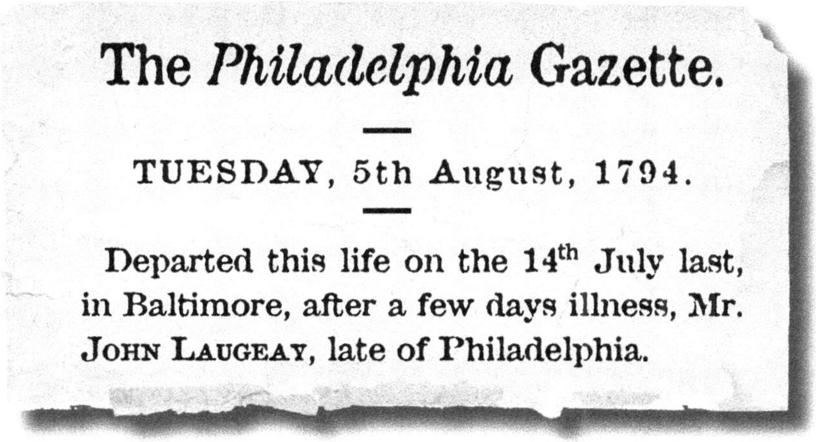

The *Philadelphia* Gazette.

—

TUESDAY, 5th August, 1794.

—

Departed this life on the 14th July last, in Baltimore, after a few days illness, Mr. JOHN LAUGEAY, late of Philadelphia.

Figure 16. Jean Laugeay dies at the height of yellow fever in Baltimore in the summer of 1794 after a short illness.

Jean had survived the Philadelphia yellow fever, and apparently moved 150 miles away, to Baltimore. However, yellow fever is known to have been particularly virulent in Baltimore in 1794. Yellow fever was likely the cause of his death at age 57.

Throughout the 1770s and 1780s, the person with the mastery to execute fireworks is Jean Laugeay. He is the only known person with such pyrotechnic knowledge near Philadelphia. He lives and works in the region and has connections with the Continental Congress. John Laugeay was the fireworker in charge of the first fireworks, held for the anniversary of the Declaration of Independence on July 4, 1777, as well as subsequent celebrations. It was only after Jean's death in 1794 that a company of "fireworkers, painters, and mechanicians" under the firm of Ambroise & Co. appeared in Philadelphia to carry on the tradition that Jean had created.

Jean, a French Huguenot and immigrant, found those of like-minded values in the Colonies. He saw our Founding Fathers speak out to forge a new philosophy of man governing without monarchies or dictators. Jean Baptiste Laugeay, as a patriot, stood tall in the name of liberty and freedom for all generations that follow. His firework displays paved the way for how we celebrate American independence to this day.

Laugeay-Lougeay Lineage

Antoine **Laugeay** and Louise Lanier

Jean Baptiste **Laugeay** a.k.a. John **Laugeay** (1736) and
Jeanne Boutin

Antoine **Laugeay** a.k.a. Anthony Lougeay (1761) and Laomi
"Amy" Yetton

John **Lougeay** (1791) and Wilhelmina Stuart Ihmsen

Dr. Charles Ihmsen **Lougeay** (1818) and Martha Ramsey

Samuel McKee **Lougeay** (1843) and Sarah A. Weston

Lawrence Weston **Lougeay** (1882) and Elsie E. Weingaertner

Howard Eugene **Lougeay** (1909) and Jean Louise Snyder

Denis Howard **Lougeay** (1943) and Denruth Colleen Barre
    Stace Michael **Lougeay** (1970) and Suzanne Hitt
    Gregg Christopher **Lougeay** (1973) and Theresa Barghols

Denruth Lougeay, PhD is a Clinical Psychologist and family genealogist. Denis Lougeay is a retired Professional Civil Engineer and business consultant. They live in Encinitas, California. Family genealogy and updates are invited. The authors can be reached at lougeay@gmail.com

www.ingramcontent.com/pod-product-compliance
Lightning Source LLC
Chambersburg PA
CBHW050824090426
42738CB00020B/3472